AMERICAN FOLK SONGS
for Guitar

Transcribed, Arranged and Edited by
David Nadal

DOVER PUBLICATIONS, INC.
Mineola, New York

ACKNOWLEDGMENTS

I am deeply indebted to many people for making this book possible:

To my parents, Will and Persephone Nadal; to my grandparents Hercules and Mary Vlassopoulos; and to my uncle Peter Vlassopoulos;

to Dominic Frasca, Allen Schulz, Kevin Gallagher, Ken Price, Greg Katavolos, David Coester, Joe Price, and Frankie Boccio for their patient ears and invaluable suggestions; and to my editor, Ronald Herder, for his help in shaping this book;

and, to the seven musicians who have contributed their finely wrought arrangements to this collection—Greg Baker, Guy Capuzzo, Mark Delpriora, Walter Jacobs, Randa Kirshbaum, Marc Mellits, and Belinda L. Reynolds— my warmest thanks and appreciation.

Bibliographical Note

David Nadal's *American Folk Songs for Guitar* is a new work, first published by Dover Publications, Inc., in 2001. His transcriptions, arrangements and editions have been specially prepared for this publication, appearing here for the first time. Works by guest arrangers appear in this collection by special permission of the writers.

International Standard Book Number: 0-486-41700-X

Manufactured in the United States of America
Dover Publications, Inc., 31 East 2nd Street, Mineola, N.Y. 11501

INTRODUCTION

When Americans think of their folk songs, they tend to think of a vast body of music familiar to themselves and their friends and neighbors. These are the songs sung to the children, learned in school, or whistled at work and play. Here is music as diverse and vital as the people from which it springs. It is a body of work that includes favorites that are generations old—often music that can be traced back to the far-away lands that were the ancestral homes of the American family. In one way or another, all the songs in this new collection form an intrinsic part of this colorful, extraordinarily diverse American culture.

Here are arrangements for guitarists at every level—from the beginning student to the concert artist. For the less experienced musician, I've added simplified chord symbols above the tablature. These will help the player to better understand the implied harmonies of the music. And, to create a less intricate, easily manageable texture in the arrangements, I've avoided the more complex inversions and extensions.

Perhaps this diversified menu of folk-song favorites—drawn from an immense body of music—will inspire the player to explore this wonderful source and the musical and performance possibilities it presents to all of us.

David Nadal
Queens, New York, 2001

David Nadal is active as a guitarist, teacher, and researcher. Dedicated to expanding the guitar repertoire, he has commissioned and premiered new works for the instrument, performing these compositions and his own arrangements and transcriptions in the United States and abroad. Recipient of degrees from both Manhattan School of Music and Yale University, David Nadal's principal guitar studies were with Tom Elliott, Nicholas Goluses, Ben Verdery, and Dominic Frasca. His most recent new editions—*Lute Songs of John Dowland, Guitar Classics,* and *Easy Classics for Guitar*—are available through Dover Publications.

He may be contacted at *david.nadal@kithara.com.*

ALPHABETICAL INDEX

All the Pretty Little Horses

Arranged by:
David Nadal

With a sad tenderness, somewhat freely (♩ = ca. 90)

Lullaby of the South

Amazing Grace

Arranged by:
Belinda L. Reynolds/Nadal

Spiritual

Flowing (♩ = 74)

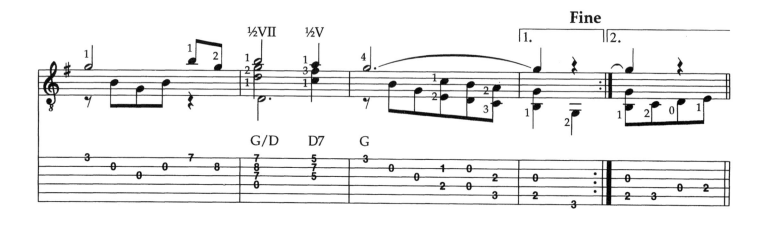

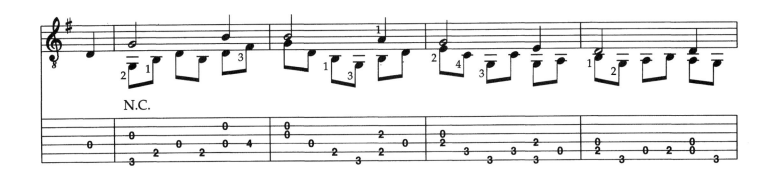

N.C.

½II

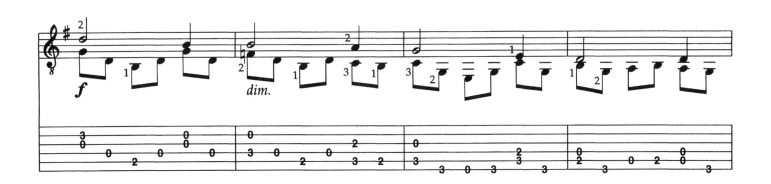

D.C. al Fine

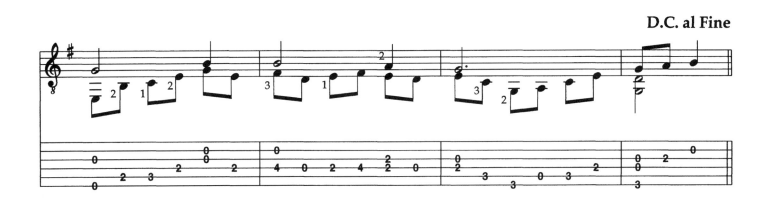

Bad Man Ballad

Arranged by:
Guy Capuzzo/Nadal

Convict Ballad

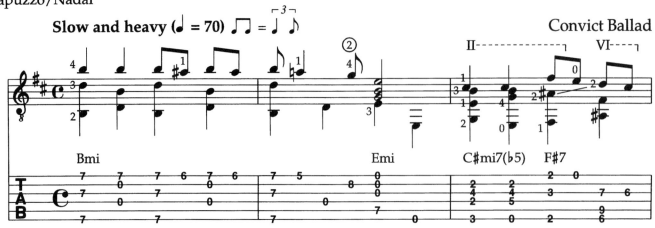

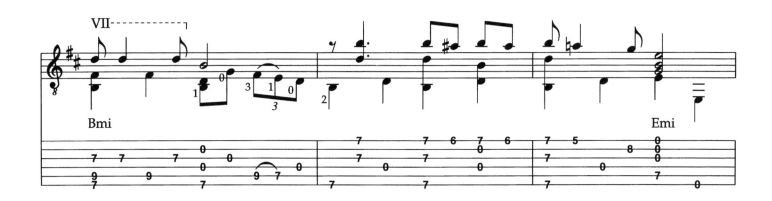

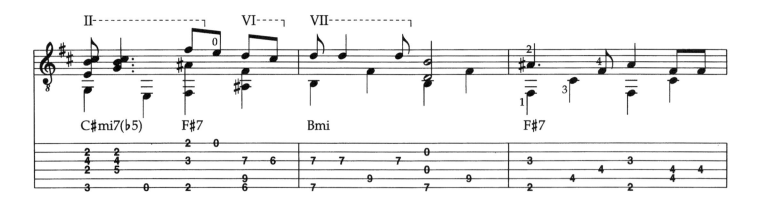

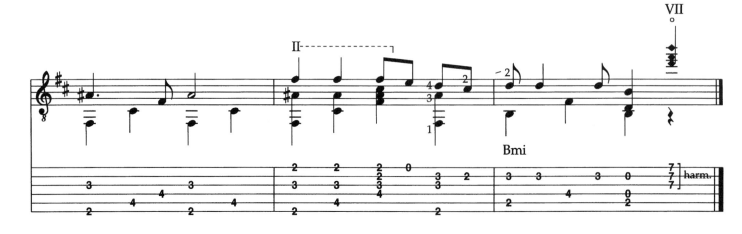

Aura Lee

Arranged by:
Marc Mellits

Serenade

Tenderly (♩ = ca. 86)

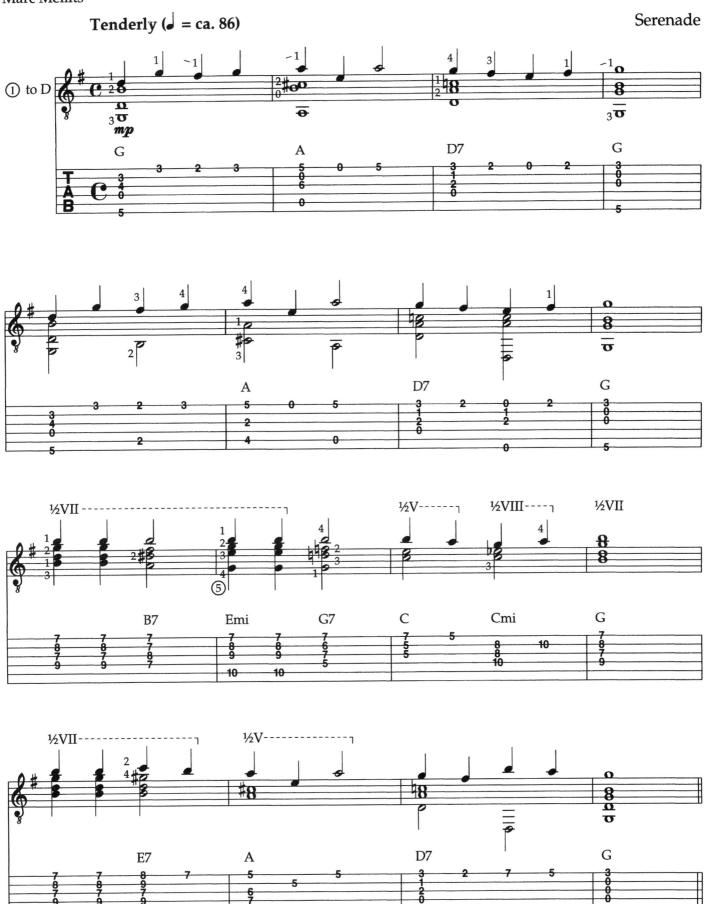

Poco più mosso
(♩ = ca. 100)

N.C.

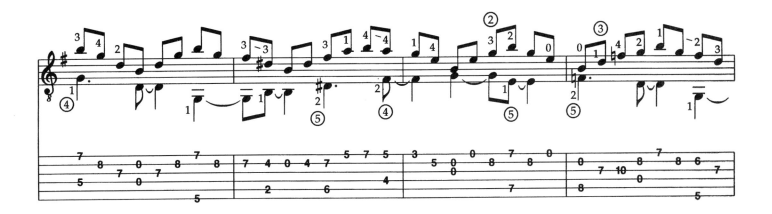

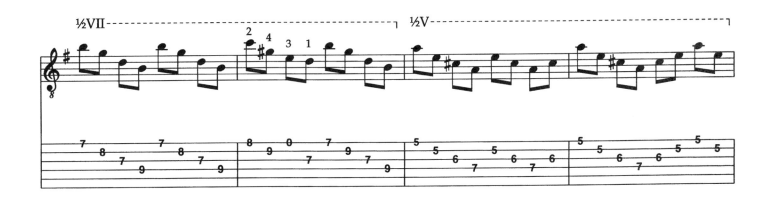

Barbara Allen

Arranged by:
Randa Kirshbaum

Gracefully (ca. ♩ = 100)

Child Ballad

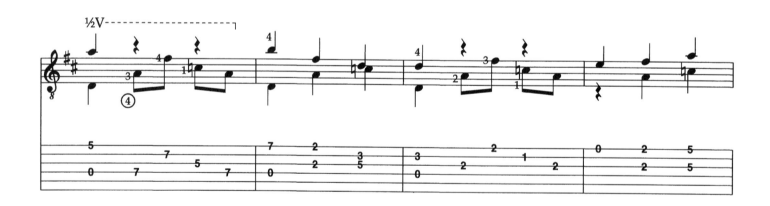

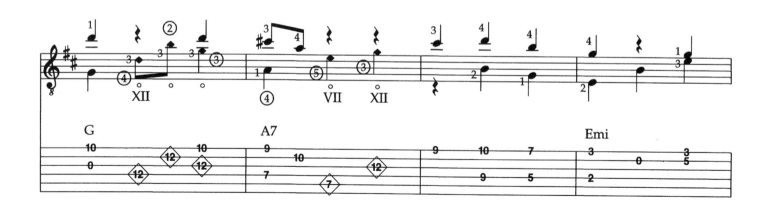

Beautiful Dreamer

Arranged by:
David Nadal

With a graceful lilt ($\bullet$. = ca. 70)

Stephen C. Foster

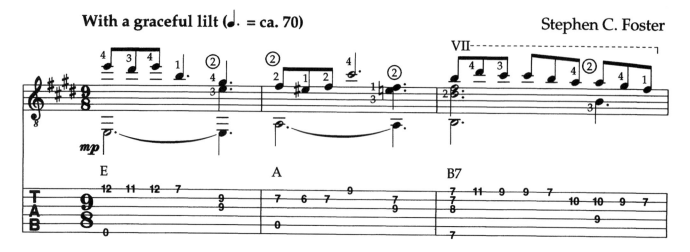

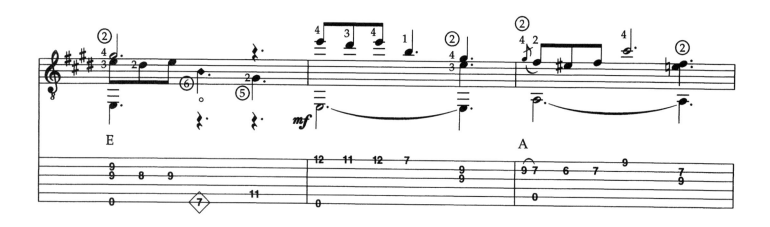

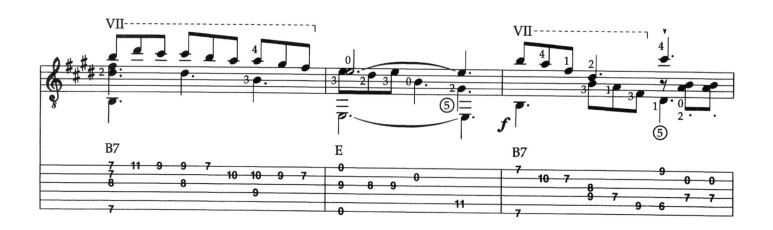

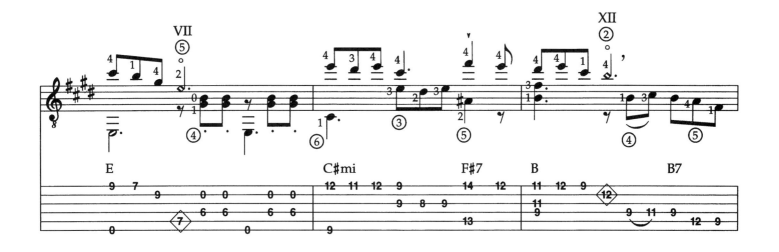

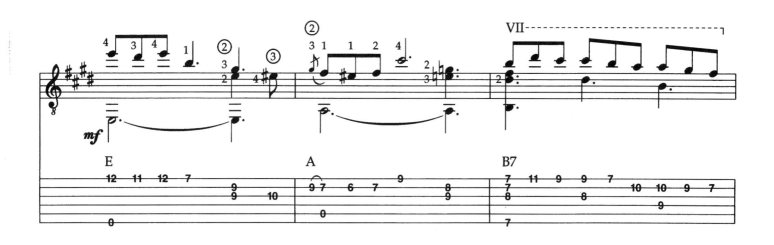

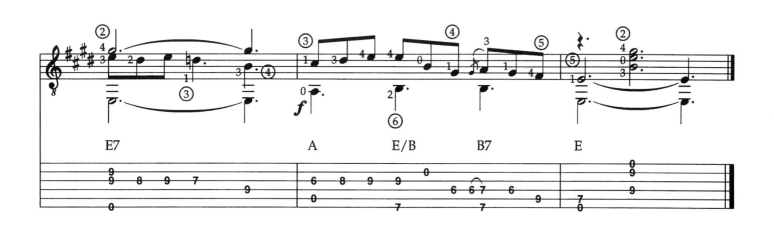

Billy Boy

Arranged by:
David Nadal

Quickly (♩ = ca. 80)

Song of the Southern Mountaineers

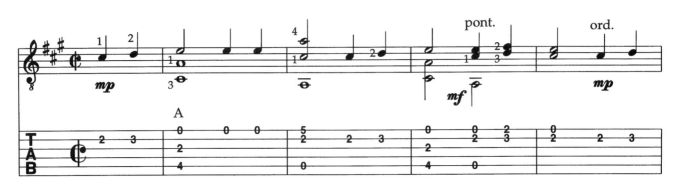

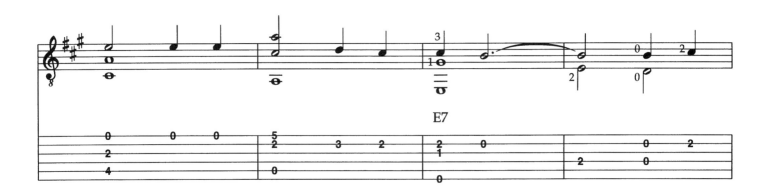

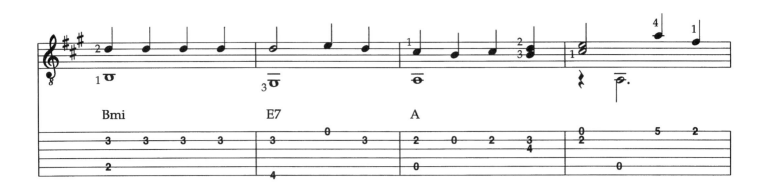

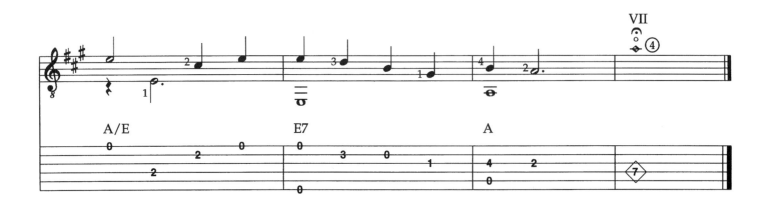

Black Is the Color

To my daughter, Mia Shan

Arranged by:
Mark Delpriora

Appalachian Song

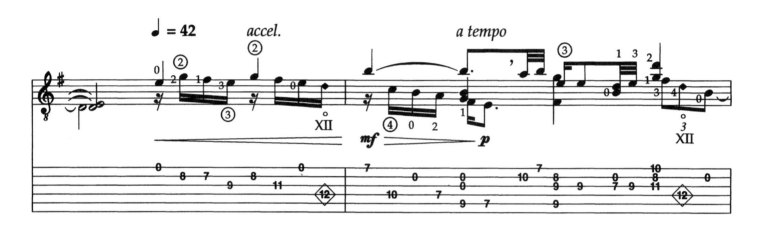

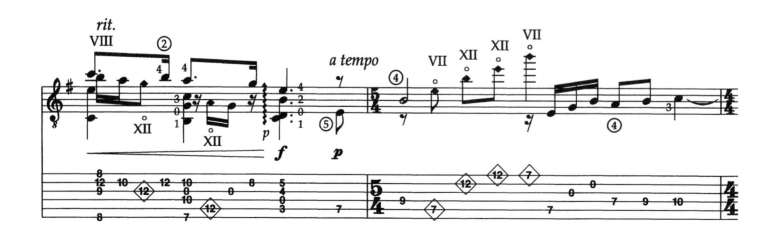

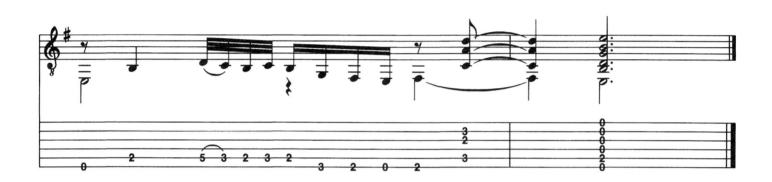

The Blood–Strained Banders

[Probably meant as "Blood–stained bandits"—a colorful image in the verse of this rare spiritual.]

Arranged by:
David Nadal

With bounce and swing (♩ =120)

Spiritual

Strum the top three strings with *i*.

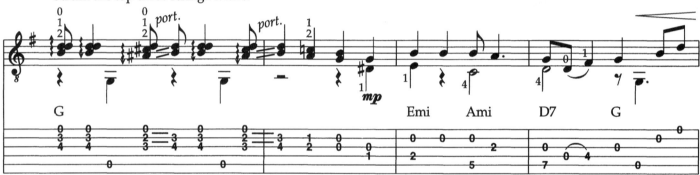

Play melody with rest–strokes, (except when strummed)

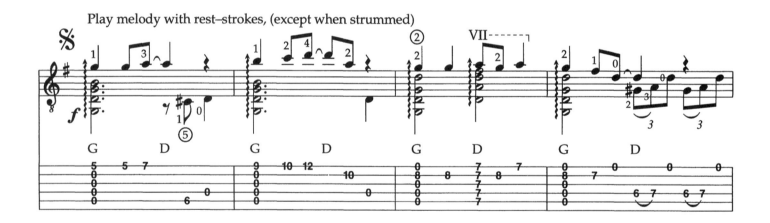

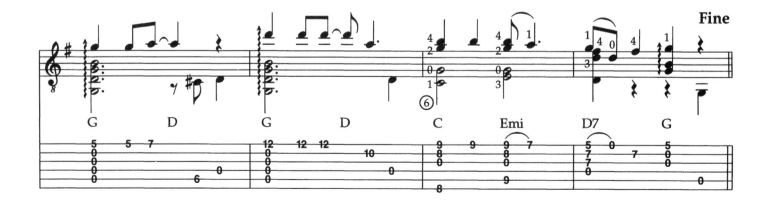

Fine

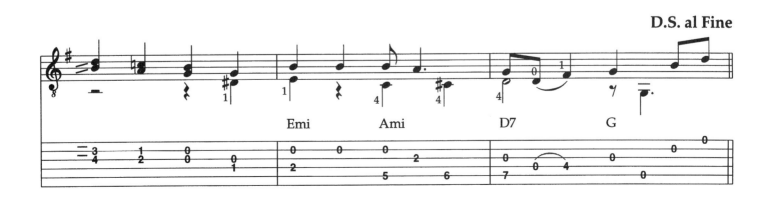

Blow the Man Down

Arranged by:
David Nadal

Sea Chanty

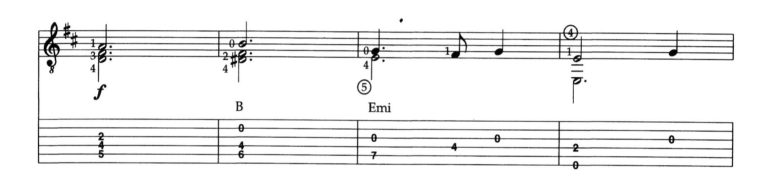

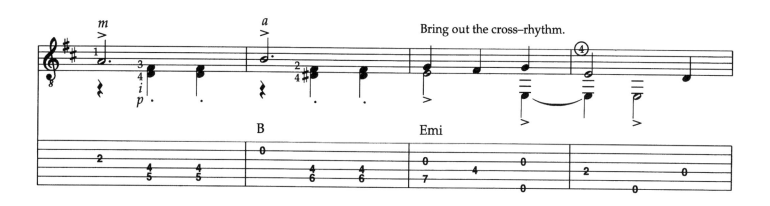

Bring out the cross–rhythm.

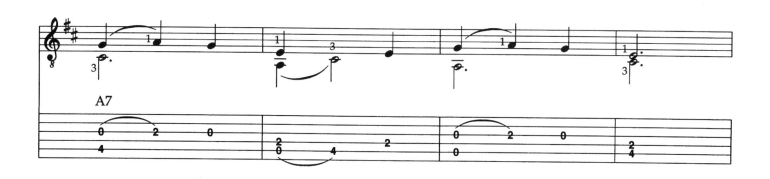

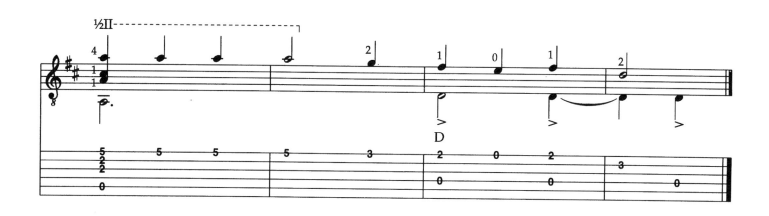

Blue Tail Fly
"Jimmy Crack Corn"

Arranged by:
David Nadal

Reflective and rhetoric (♩ = ca. 100)

Minstrel Song

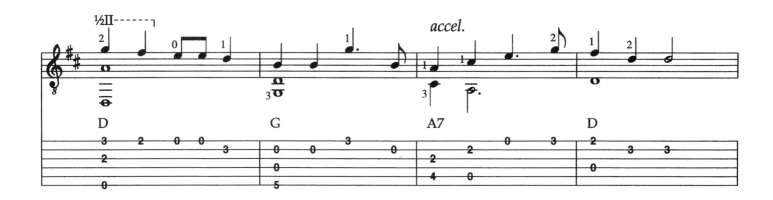

In time (♩ = ca. 140)

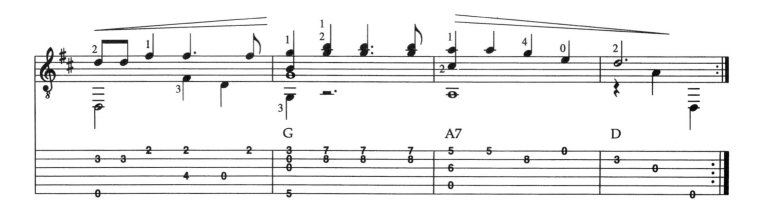

Brother John

Arranged by:
David Nadal

Simply and clearly (♩ = 88)

Children's Round

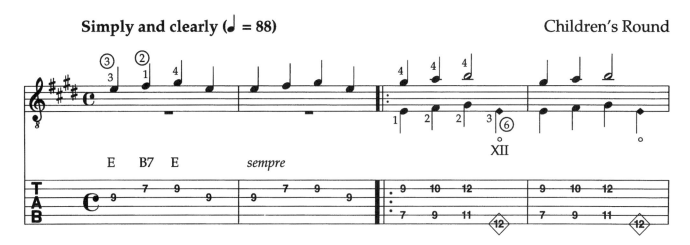

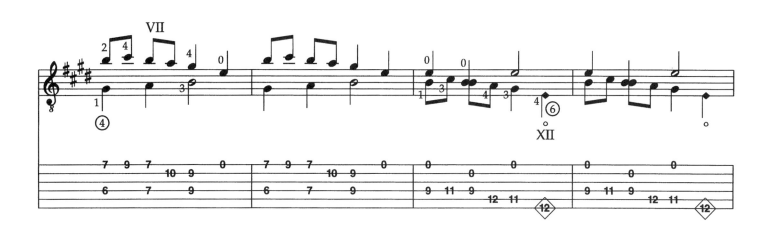

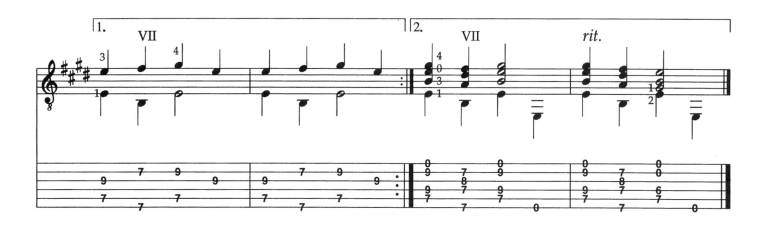

Camptown Races

Arranged by:
David Nadal

Stephen C. Foster

Cheerfully (♩ = 80)

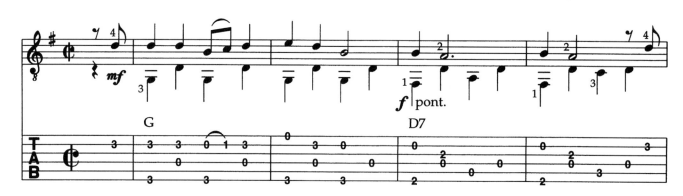

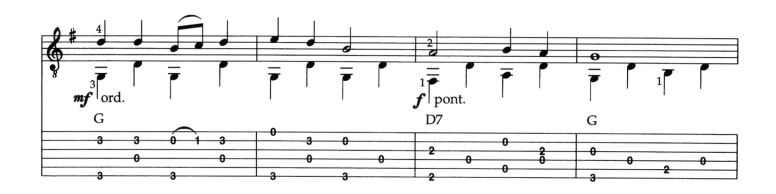

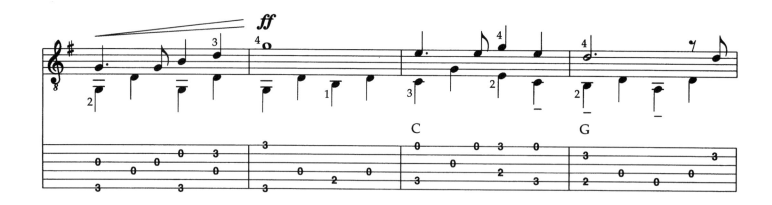

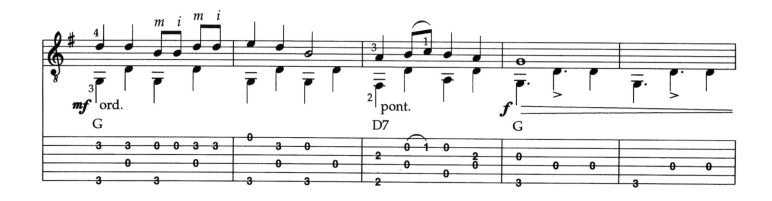

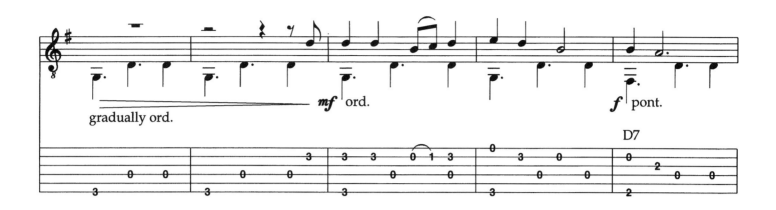

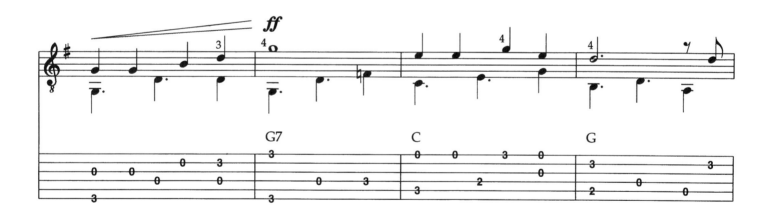

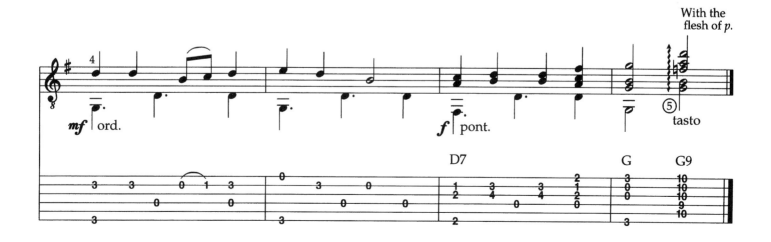

Careless Love

Arranged by:
David Nadal

Kentucky Mountains

Waltz (♩. = 50)

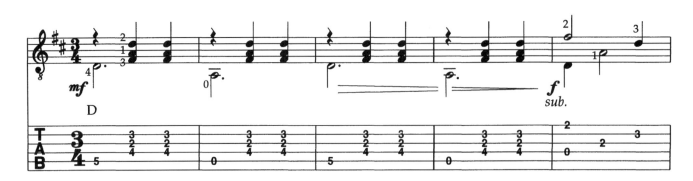

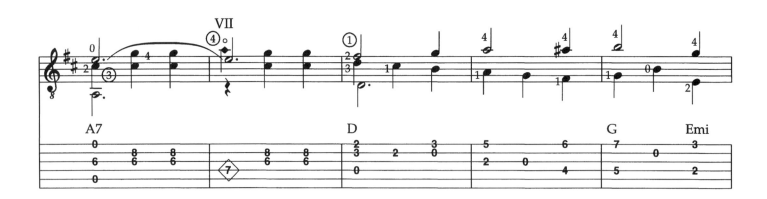

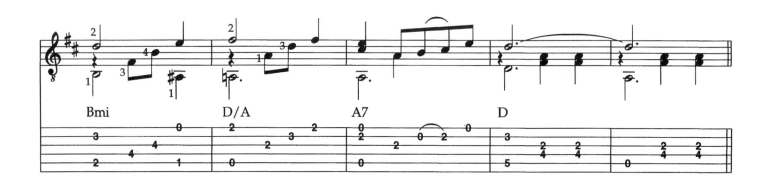

Charlie Is My Darling

Arranged by:
David Nadal

Playfully, but with a certain sense of tragedy (♩. = ca. 108)

New England Ballad

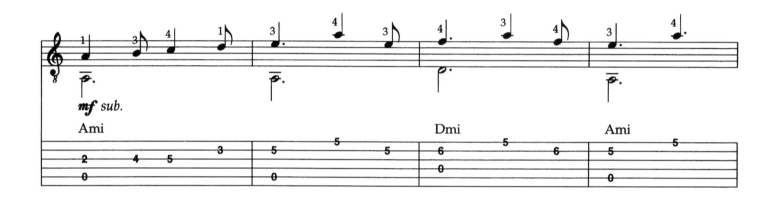

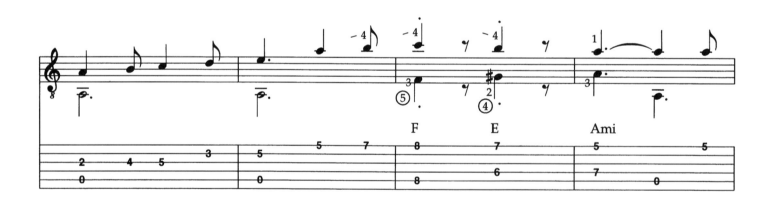

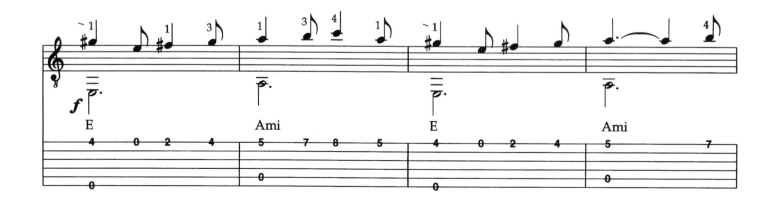

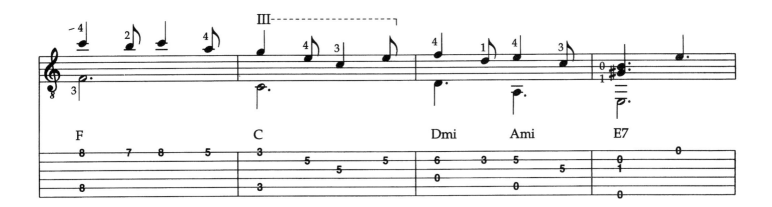

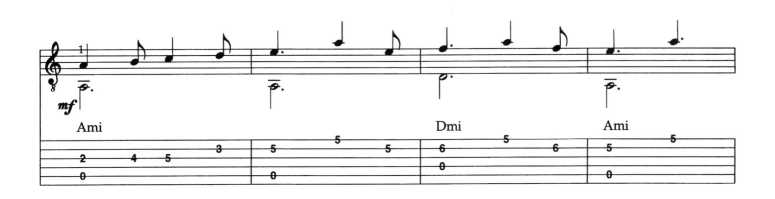

Buffalo Gals

Arranged by:
David Nadal

Square Dance

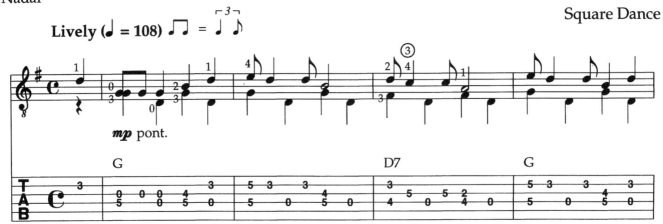

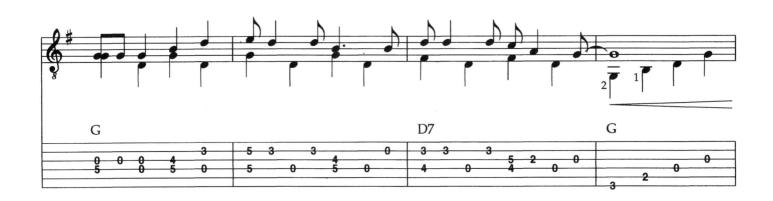

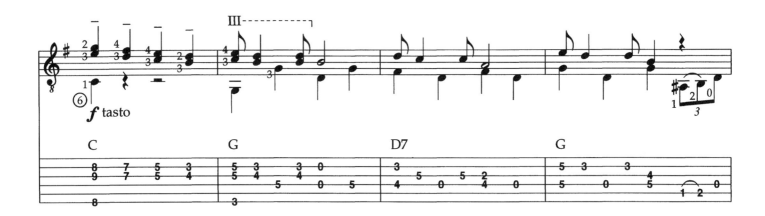

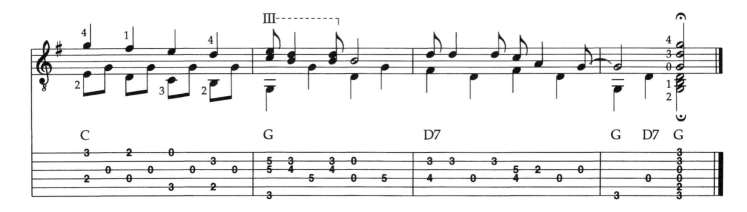

Clementine

Arranged by:
David Nadal

Flowing, sadly (♩ = 74)

Percy Montross

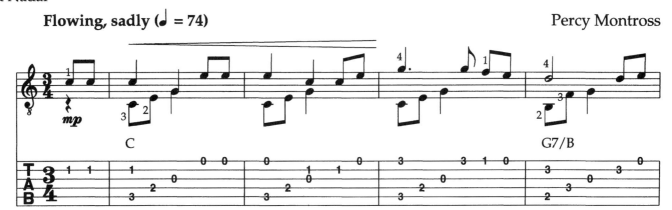

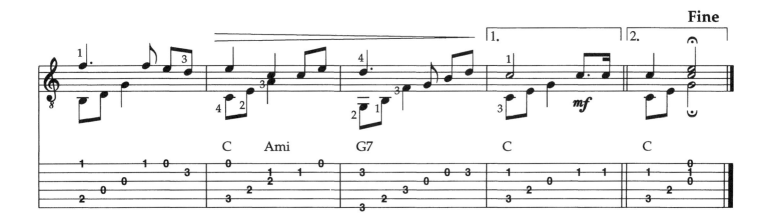

Cumberland Gap

Arranged by:
David Nadal

Quickly and with spirit (♩ = 80)

Appalachian Song

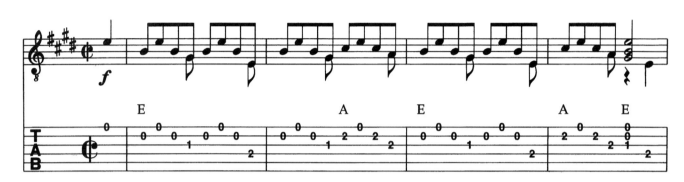

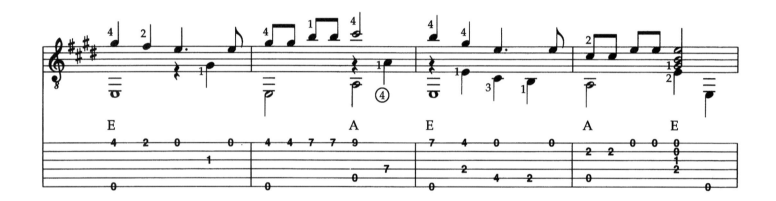

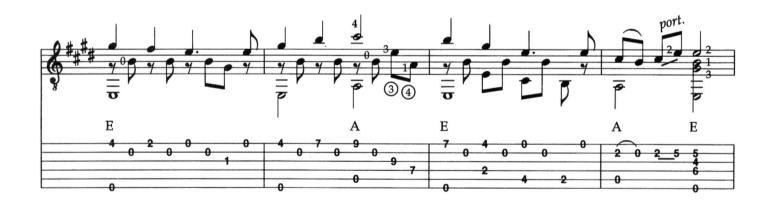

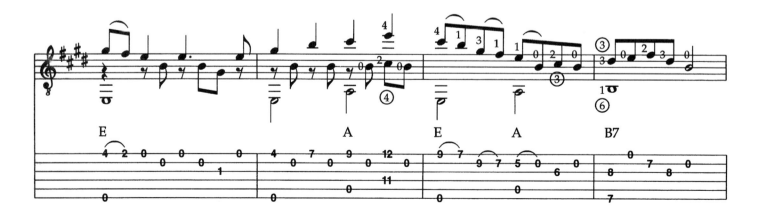

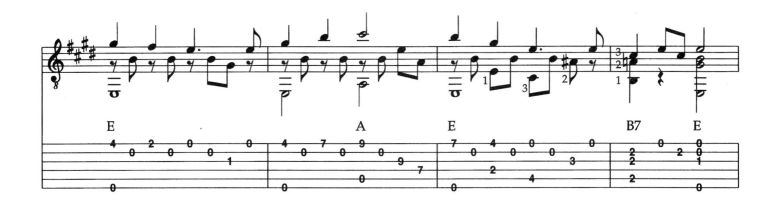

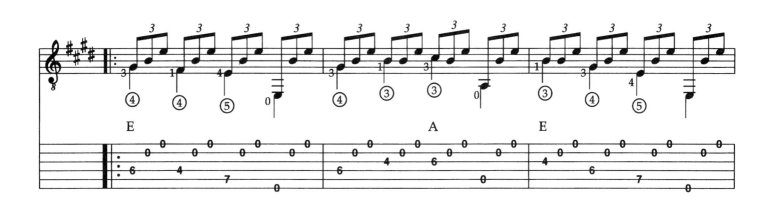

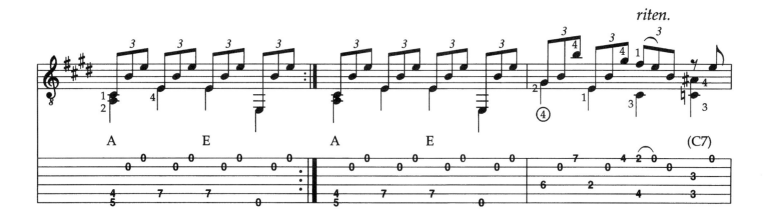

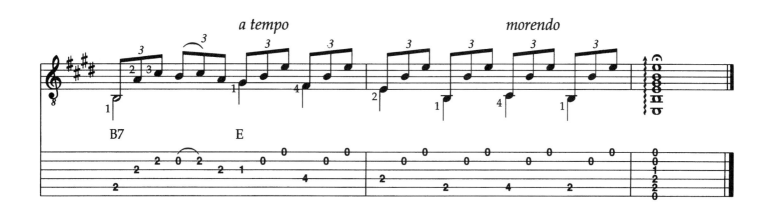

Deep River

Arranged by:
David Nadal

Spiritual

Slowly (= 66)

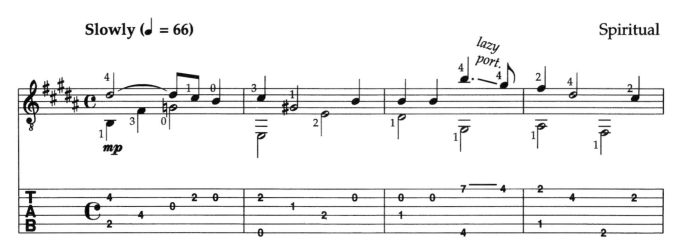

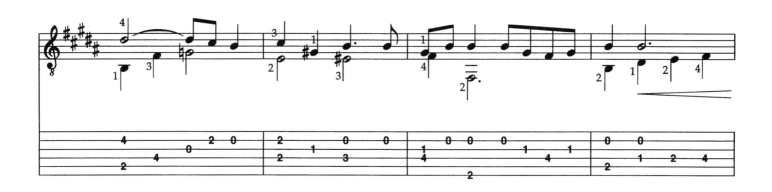

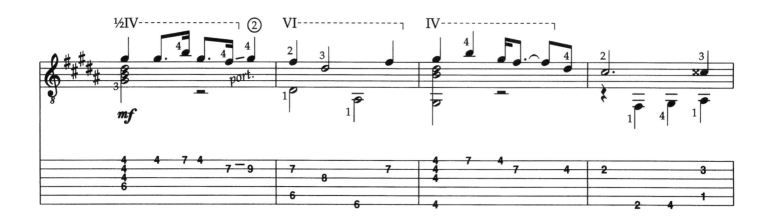

Down by the Riverside

Arranged by:
David Nadal

Spiritual

Swaying along (♩ = ca. 92)

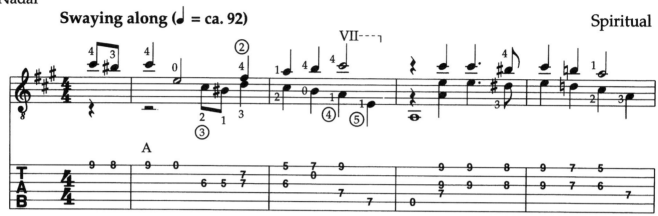

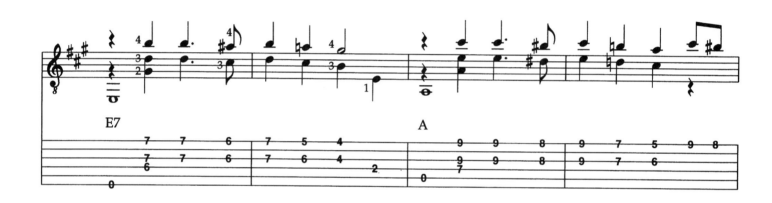

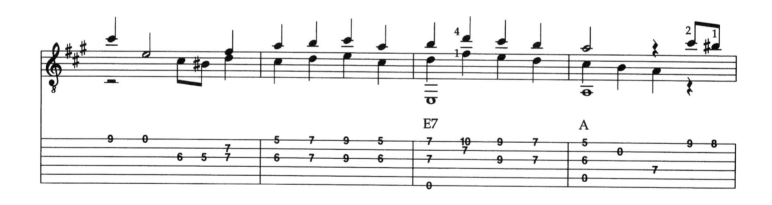

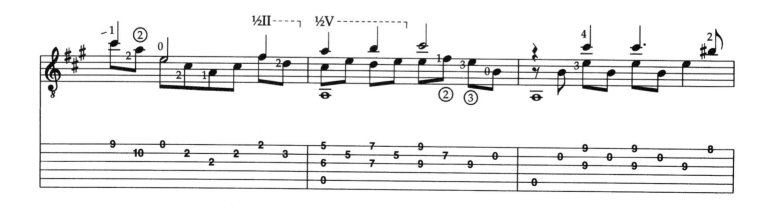

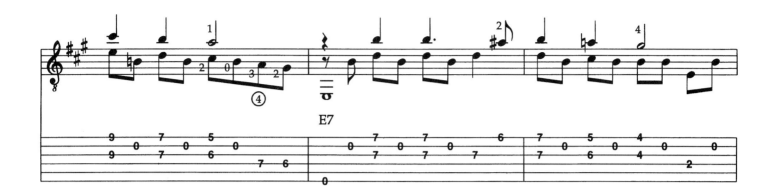

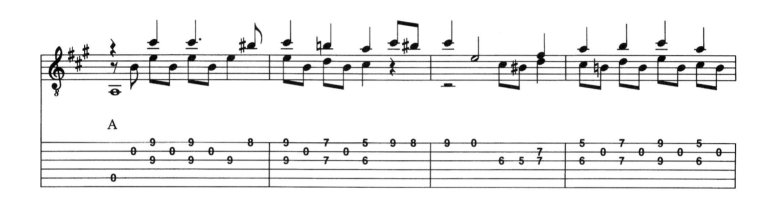

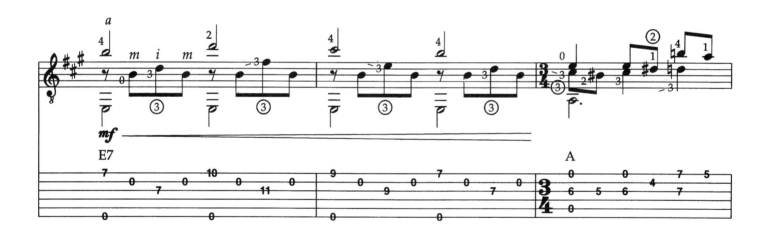

Down in the Valley

Arranged by:
David Nadal

Appalachian Serenade

** *ossia*

* The performer is encouraged to improvise an introduction.

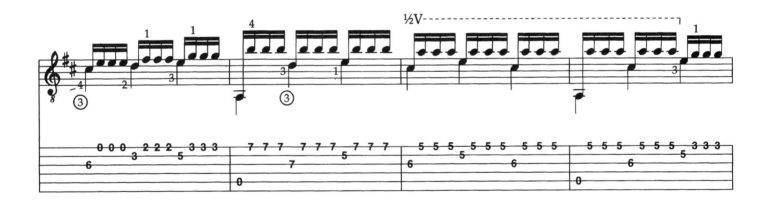

Go Down, Moses

Arranged by:
David Nadal

Spiritual

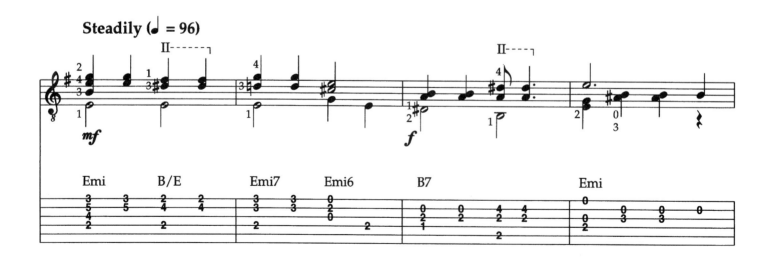

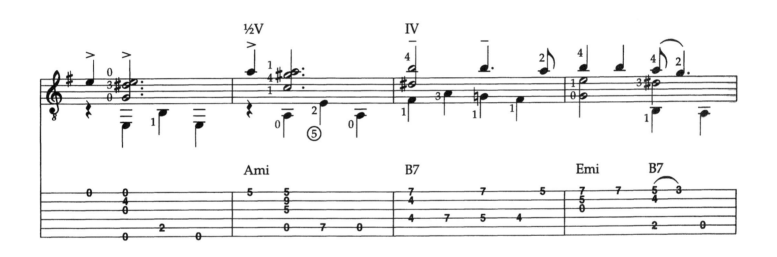

Go Tell Aunt Rhody

Arranged by:
David Nadal

Children's Song

Sweetly (♩ = ca. 88)

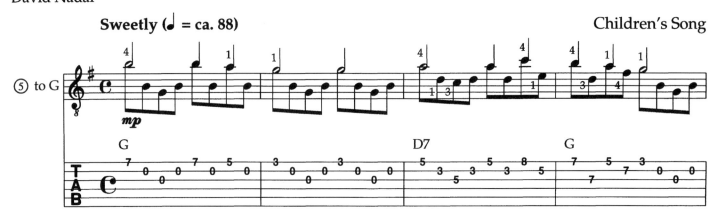

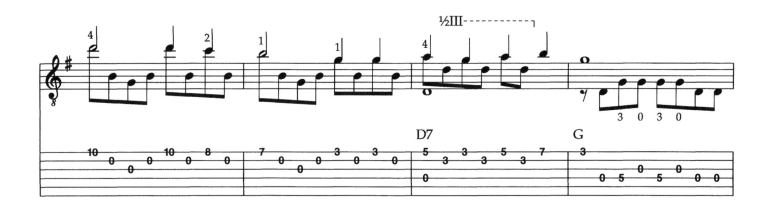

Always on the beat.

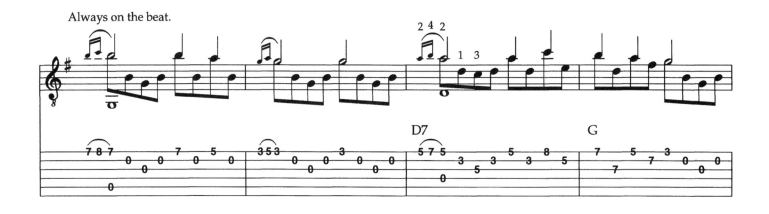

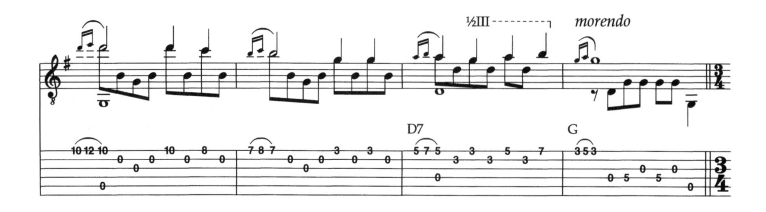

Mechanically (♩ = ♩ throughout)

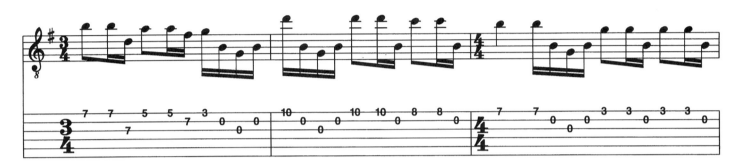

Home on the Range

Arranged by:
Greg Baker

Gracefully (♩ = ca. 88)

Cowboy Song

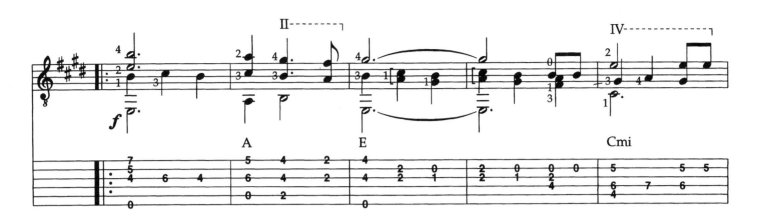

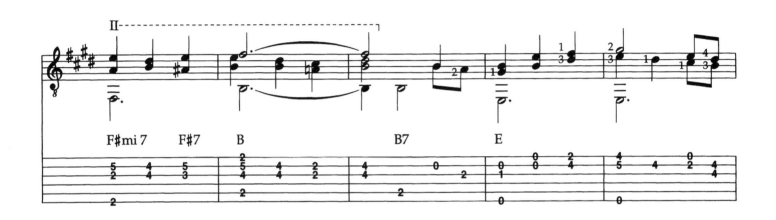

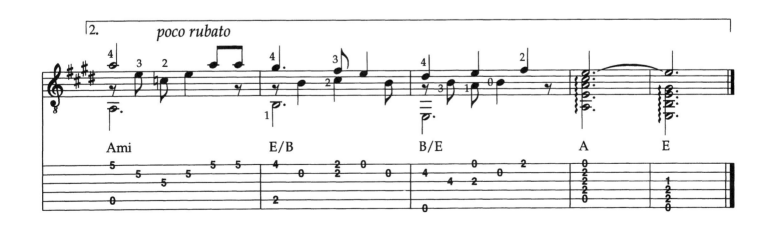

Hush, Little Baby

Arranged by:
David Nadal

Tenderly (♩ = ca. 88)

Appalachian Lullaby

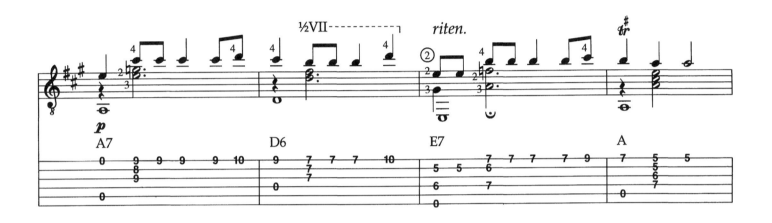

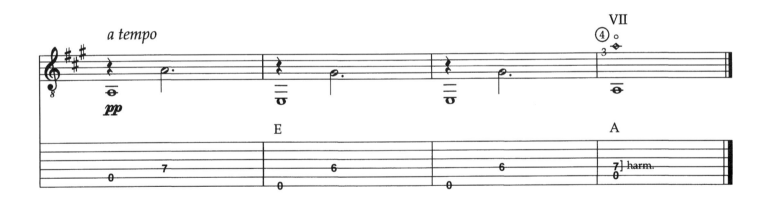

Jeanie with the Light Brown Hair

Arranged by:
David Nadal

Lyrically, not too fast (♩ = ca. 80)

Stephen C. Foster

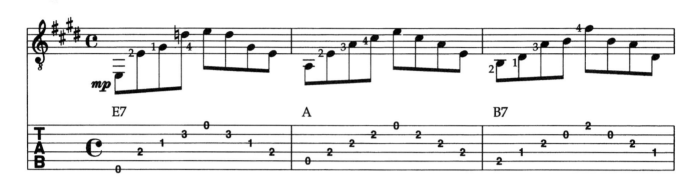

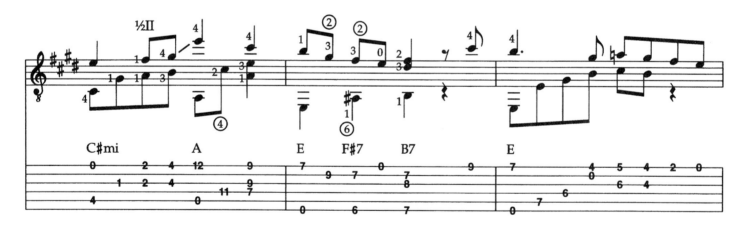

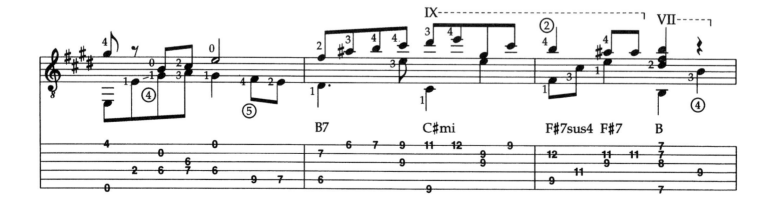

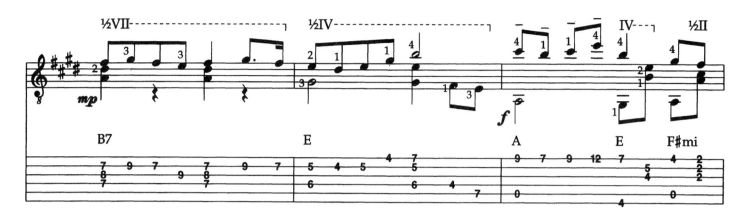

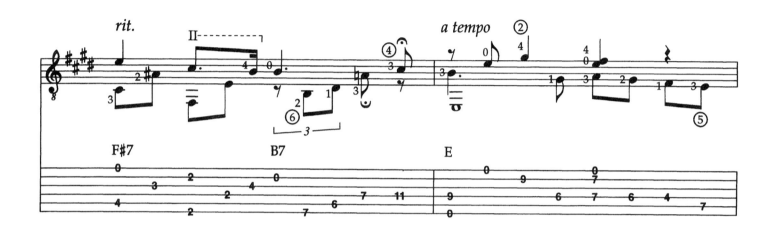

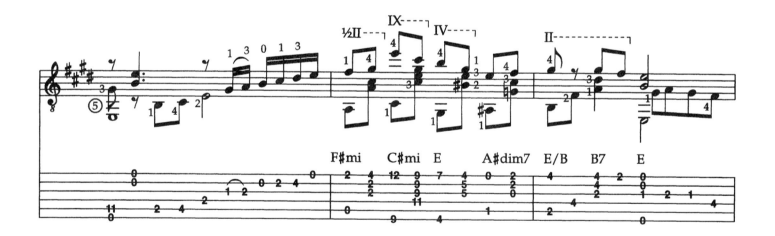

John Henry

Arranged by:
David Nadal

Bright, heavy and soulful (♩ = 120)

Work Ballad

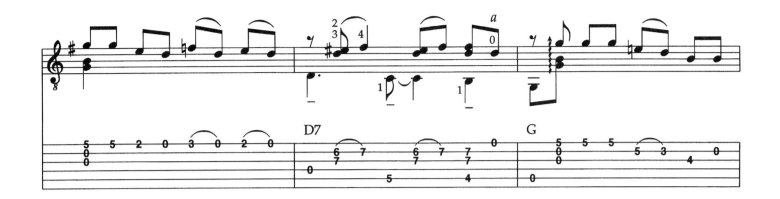

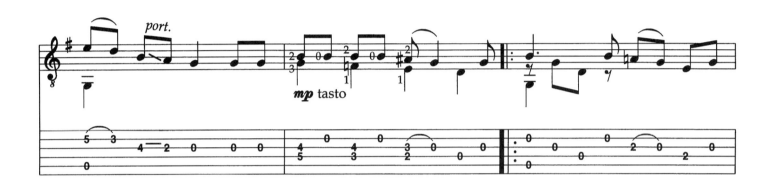

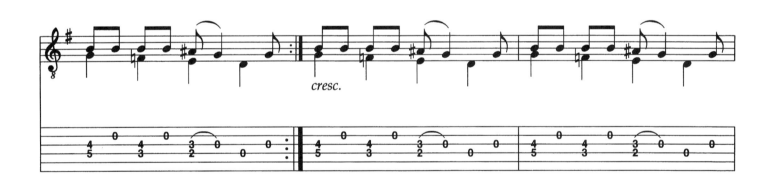

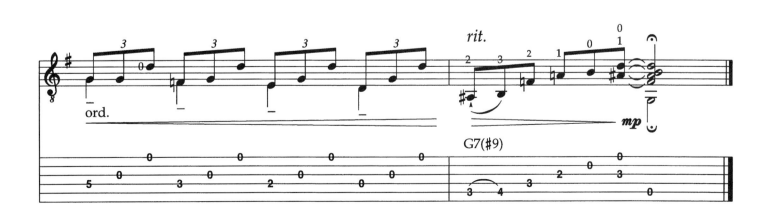

I've Been Workin' on the Railroad

Arranged by:
David Nadal

Bright and well measured (♩ = 120)

Work Song

Play the melody with *p*.

Little Brown Jug

Arranged by:
David Nadal

Merrily (♩ = 80)

Drinking Song

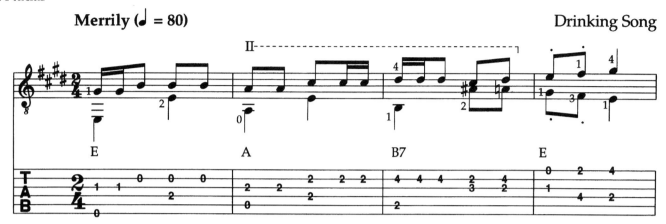

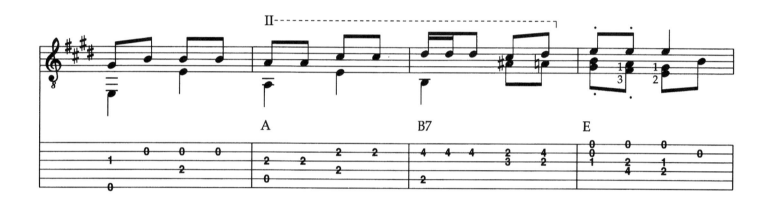

My Old Kentucky Home

Arranged by:
Walter Jacobs

Stephen C. Foster

Nostalgically (♩ = 76)

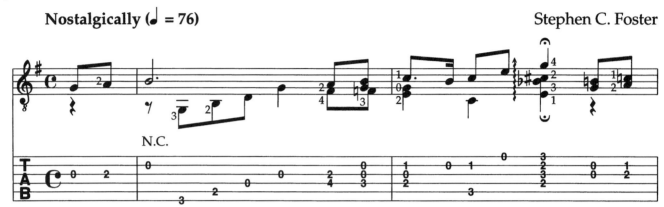

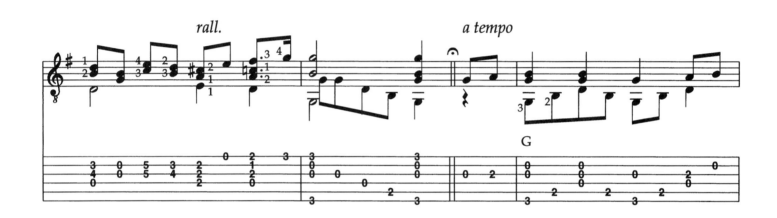

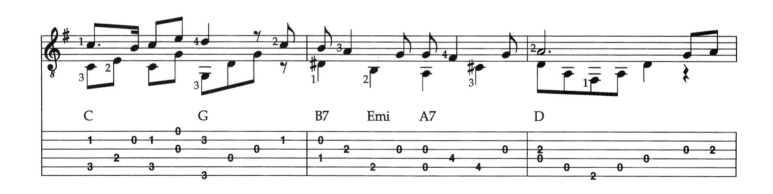

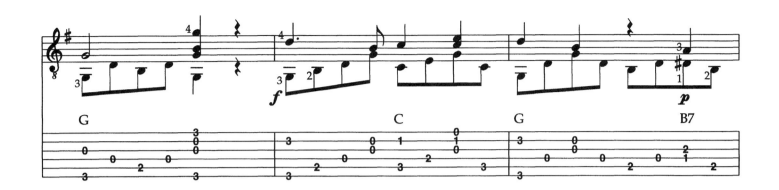

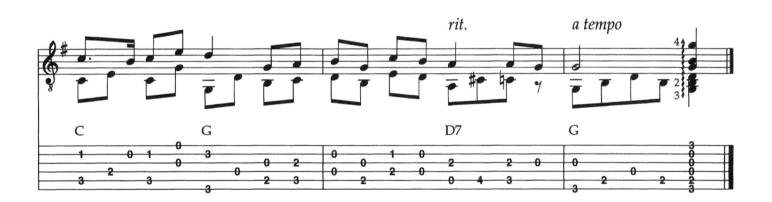

Oh! Susanna

Arranged by:
David Nadal

Stephen C. Foster

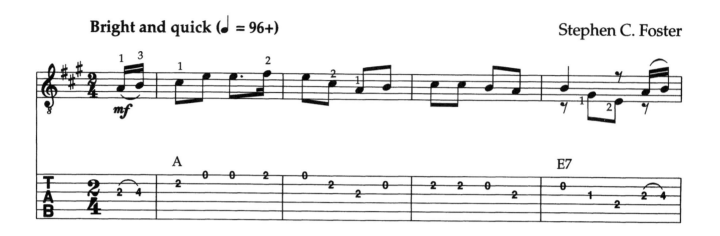

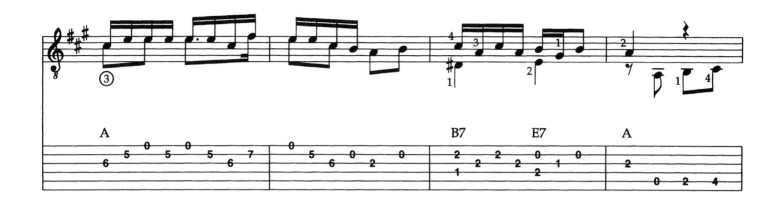

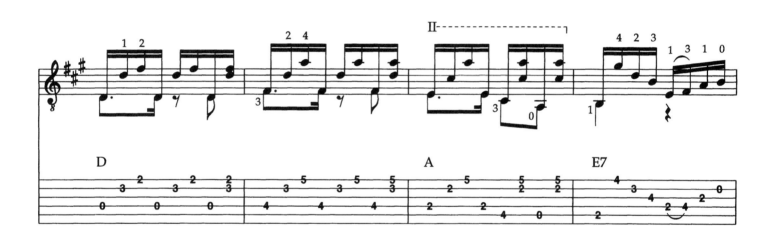

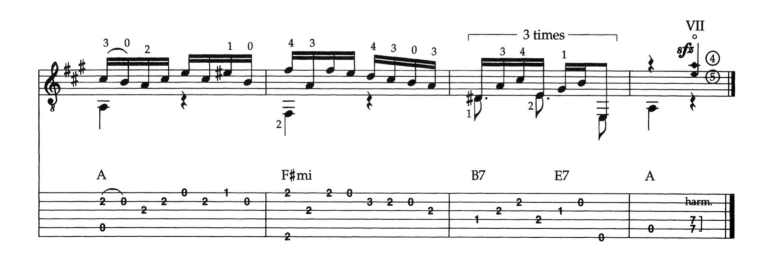

Never Said a Mumblin' Word

Arranged by:
David Nadal

Spiritual

Dark, mournful and heavy (♩ = ca. 80)

Polly Wolly Doodle

Arranged by:
David Nadal

Minstrel Song

With spirit (♩ = 80)

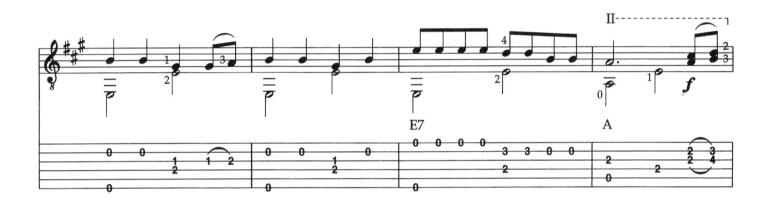

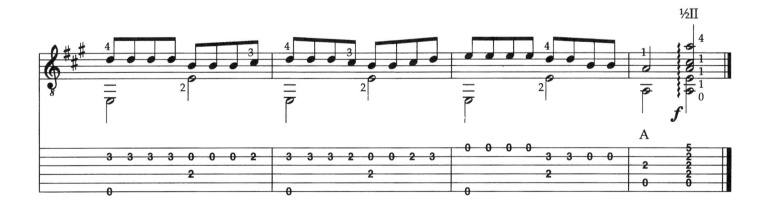

Pop Goes the Weasel

Arranged by:
David Nadal

Playfully ($\sqrt{} . = 104$)

Children's Singing Game

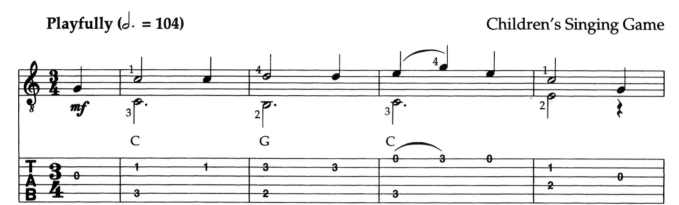

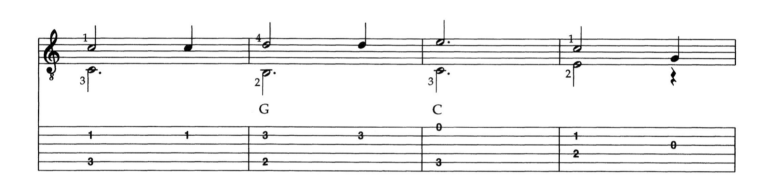

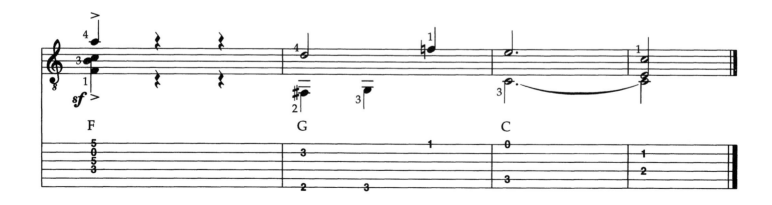

Rémon

Arranged by:
David Nadal

Creole Song

With a lilt (♩ = 72)

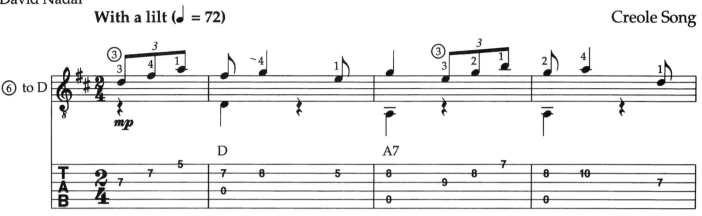

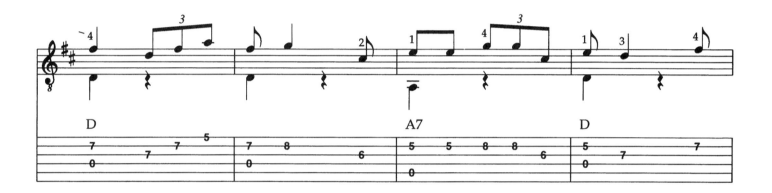

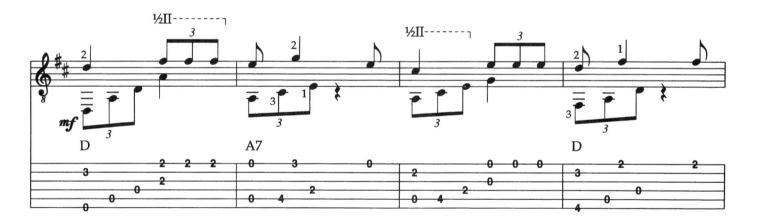

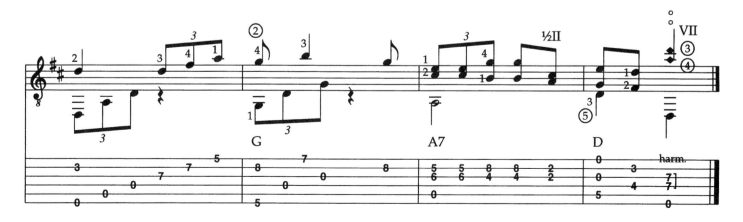

She'll Be Comin' 'Round the Mountain

Bright (♩ = 100+)

Railroad Song

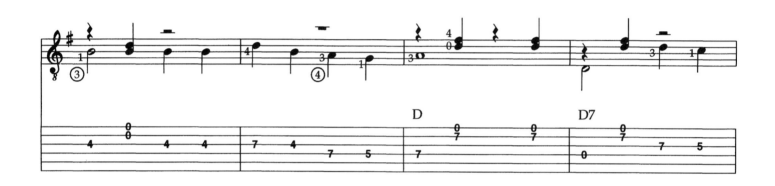

She'll Be Comin' 'Round the Mountain

"The Encore Version"

Arranged by:
David Nadal

Railroad Song

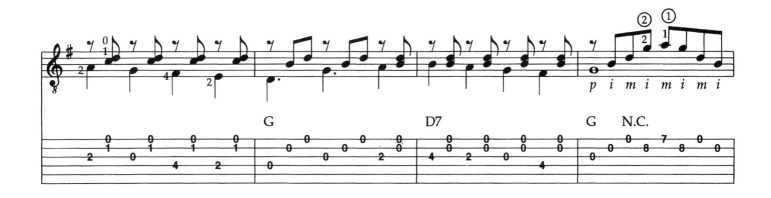

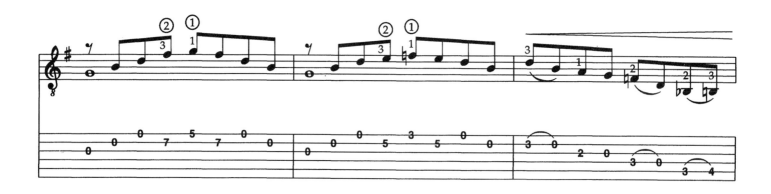

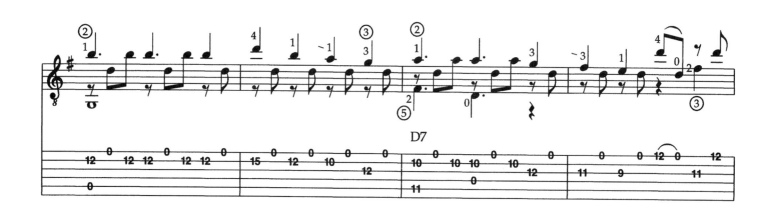

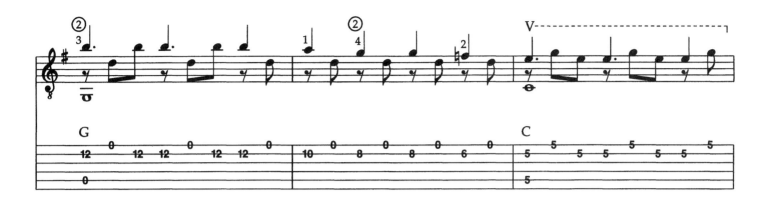

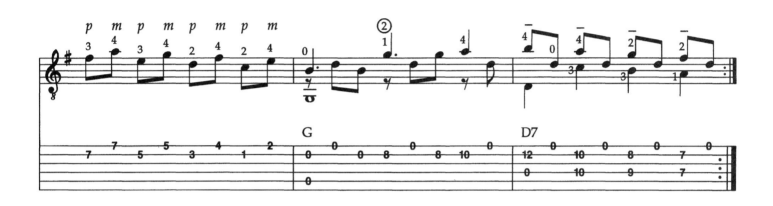

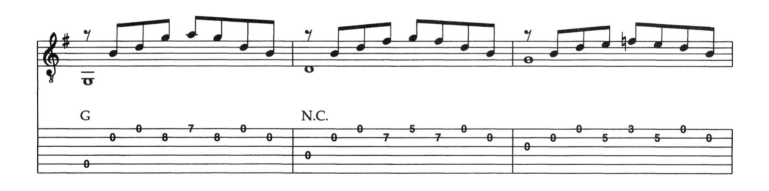

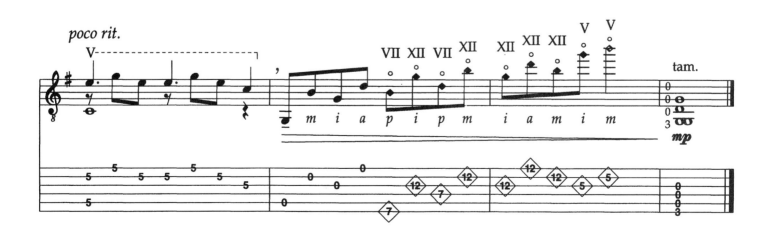

Shenandoah

Arranged by:
David Nadal

Appalachian Ballad

Slowly and lyrically (ca. ♩ = 72)

65

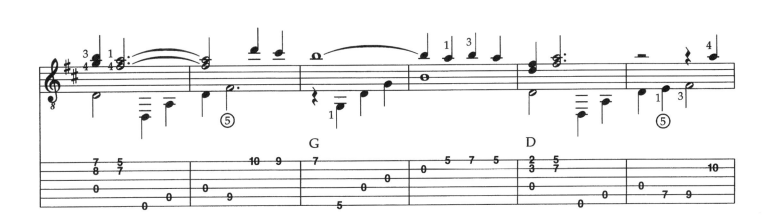

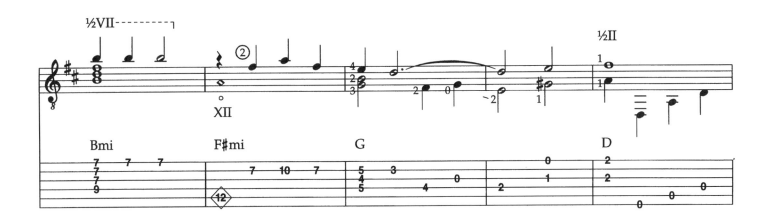

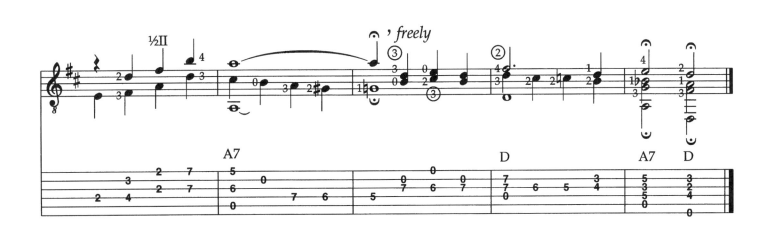

Shortnin' Bread

Arranged by:
David Nadal

Song of the South

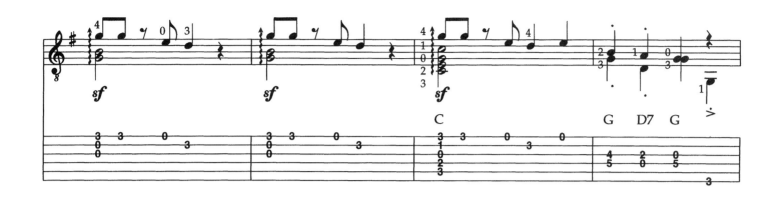

Simple Gifts

Arranged by:
David Nadal

Shaker Hymn

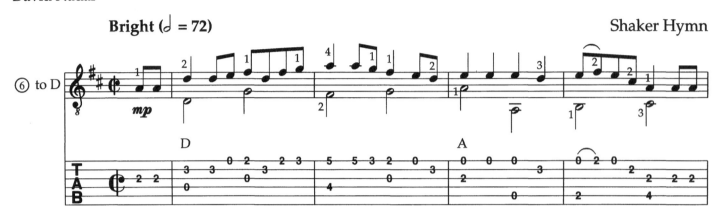

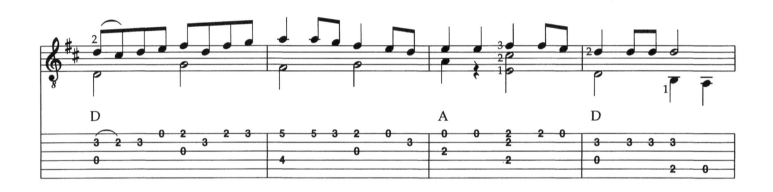

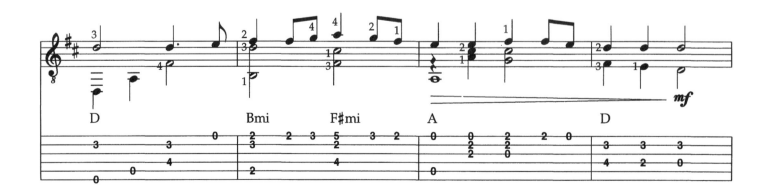

Skip to My Lou

Arranged by:
David Nadal

Play Song

Sometimes I Feel Like a Motherless Child

Arranged by:
David Nadal

Mournfully and rhetorically

Spiritual

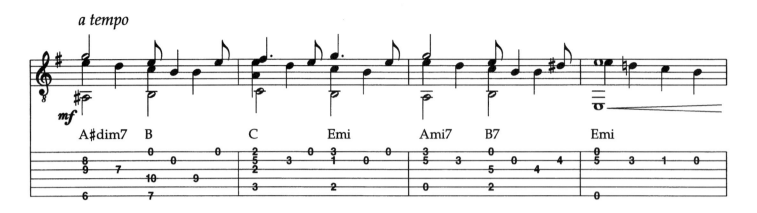

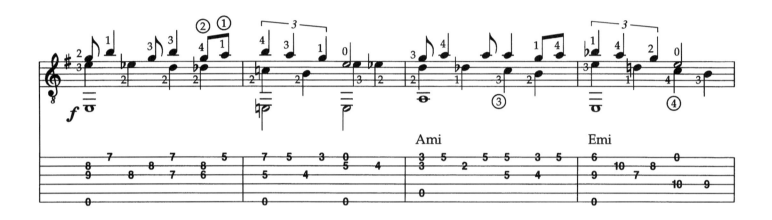

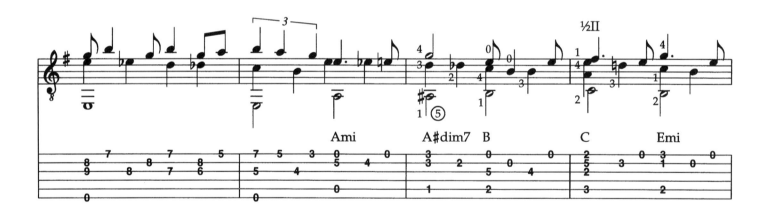

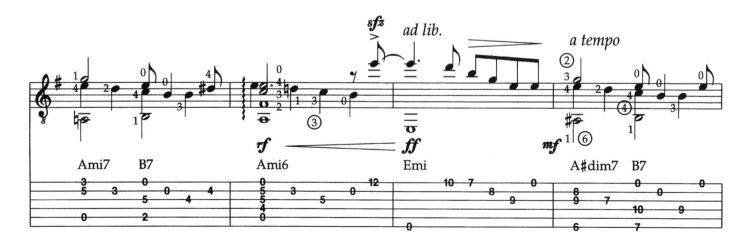

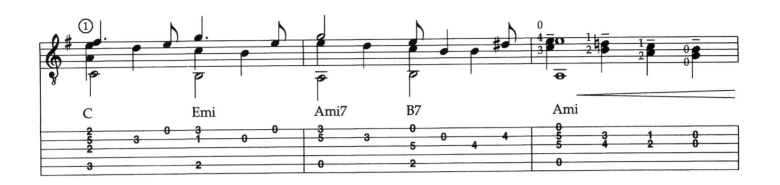

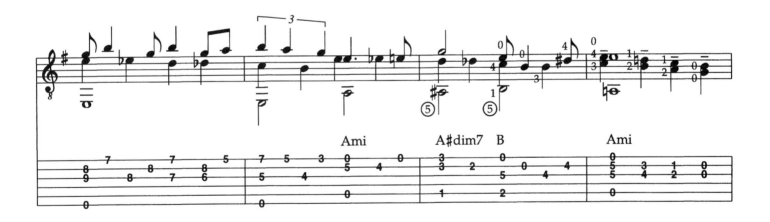

Streets of Laredo

Arranged by:
David Nadal

Reflective and sad (♩ = ca. 94)

Cowboy Ballad

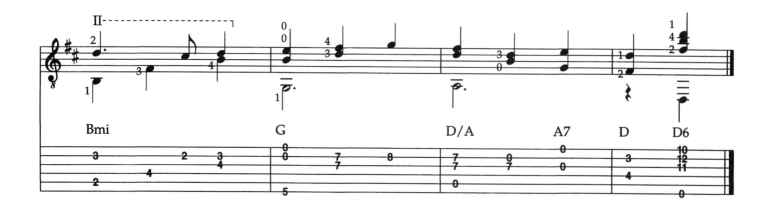

Sweet Betsy from Pike

Arranged by:
David Nadal

Playfully (♩. = 75)

Song of the Gold Rush Pioneers

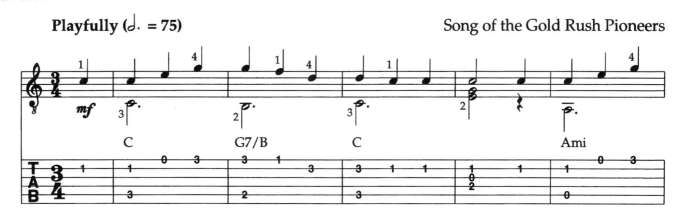

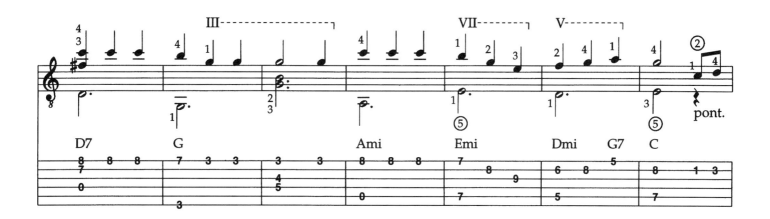

Turkey in the Straw

Arranged by:
David Nadal

Appalachian Fiddle Tune

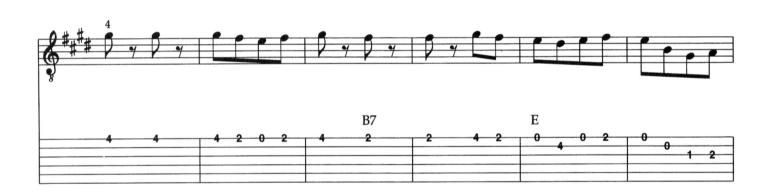

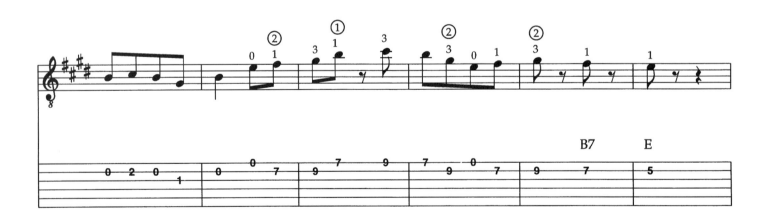

Hammer on with force to get the top note to sound.

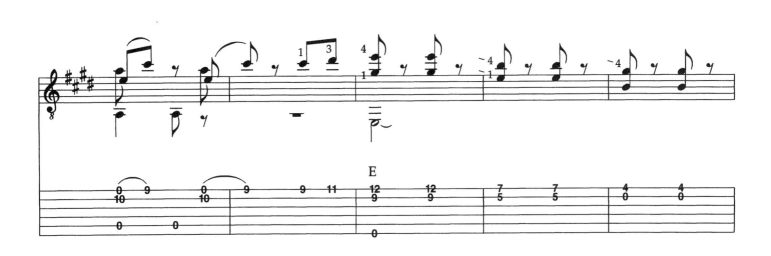

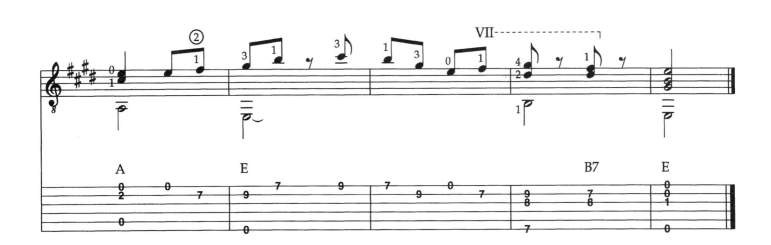

Thanksgiving Prayer

Arranged by:
David Nadal

Reverently (♩ = ca. 89)

Colonial Congregational Hymn

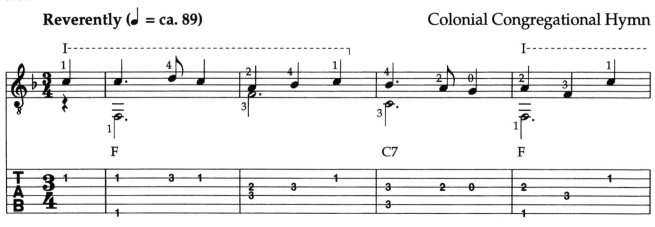

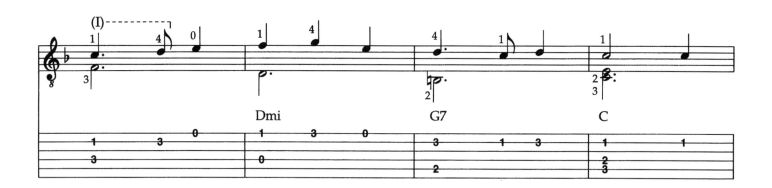

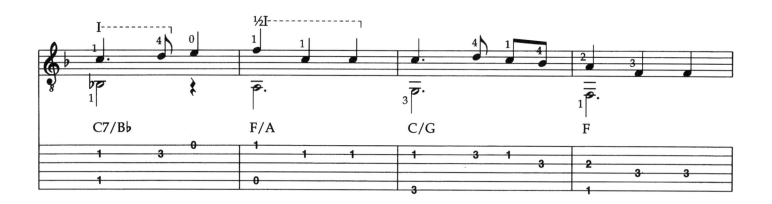

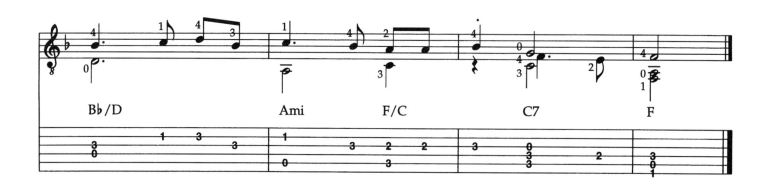

Wayfaring Stranger

Arranged by:
David Nadal

Not fast (♩ = ca. 96)

Appalachian Lament

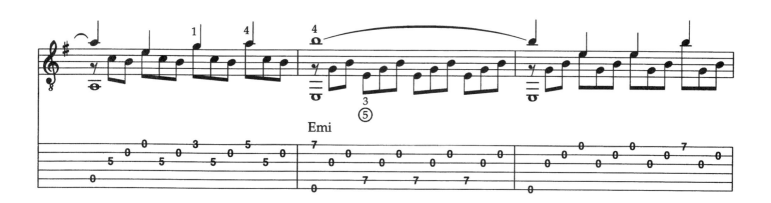

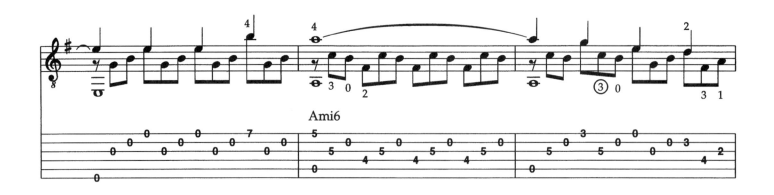

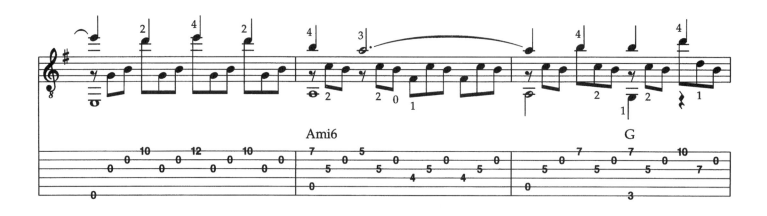

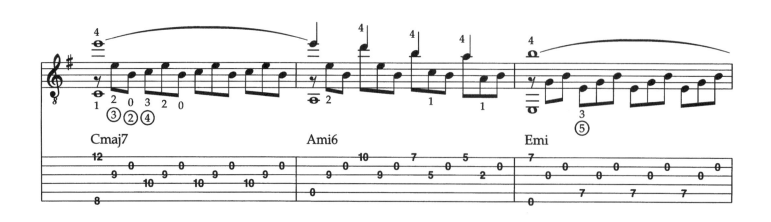

When Johnny Comes Marching Home

Arranged by:
David Nadal

Glorious and mean (♩. = 100)

Patrick S. Gilmore

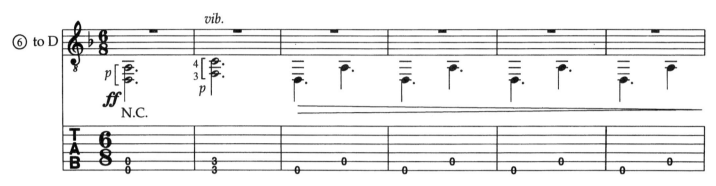

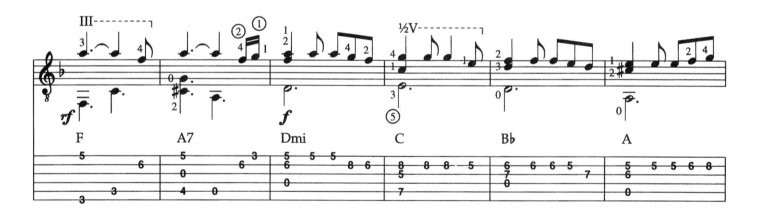

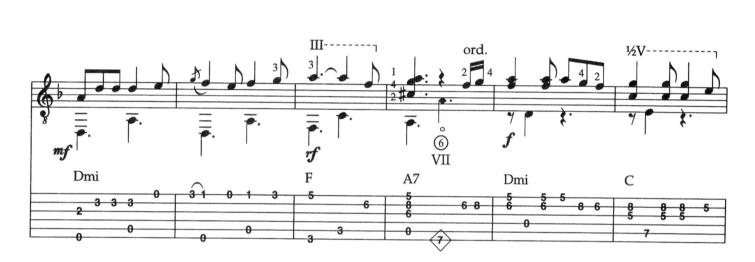

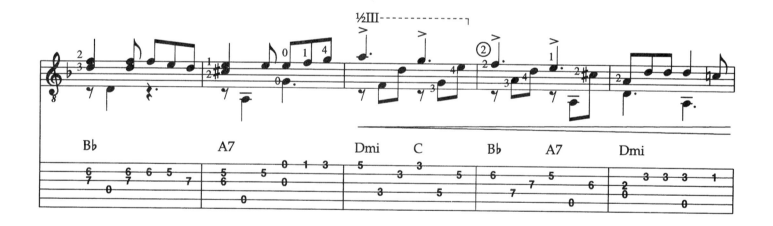

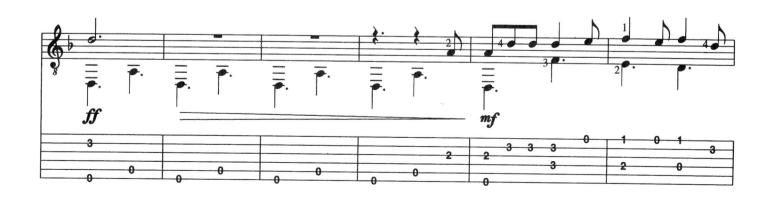

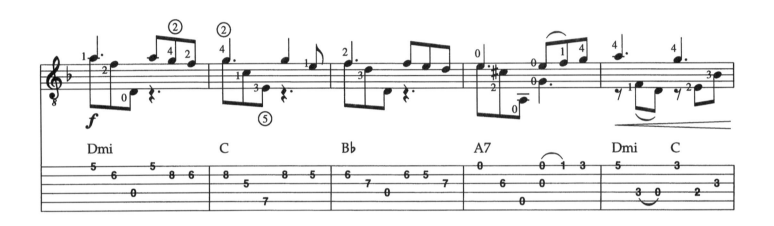

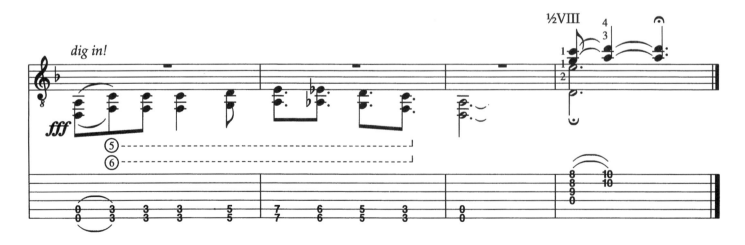

Yankee Doodle

Arranged by:
David Nadal

Revolutionary War Song

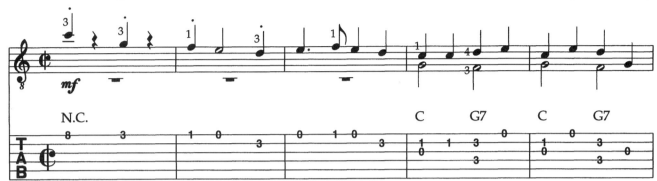

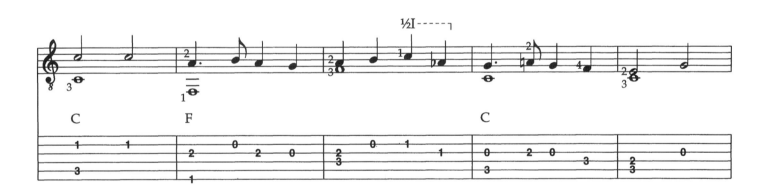

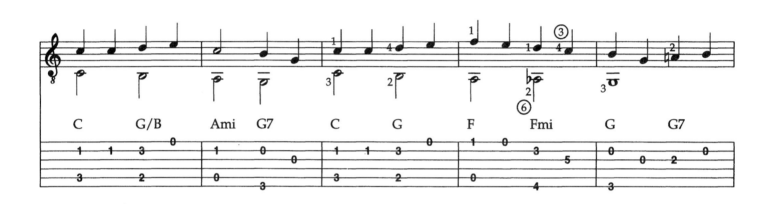

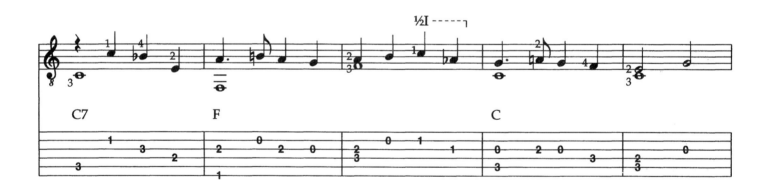

Amazing Grace

For Two Guitars

Spiritual

Black–eyed Susie

For Two Guitars

Arranged by:
David Nadal

Appalachian Fiddle Tune

Fast (♩ = 124+)